RAISED

from the

OTHER SIDE

Jody Lutzke

BALBOA.
PRESS
A DIVISION OF HAY HOUSE

Balboa Press books may be ordered through booksellers or by contacting:

Balboa Press
A Division of Hay House
1663 Liberty Drive
Bloomington, IN 47403
www.balboapress.com
1 (877) 407-4847

Print information available on the last page.

ISBN: 978-1-5043-9970-8 (sc)
ISBN: 978-1-5043-9969-2 (e)

Balboa Press rev. date: 02/27/2018

Acknowledgments

Mom and Dad, thank you for being by my side and guiding me as I wrote this book. It is because of the strength that you have given me that I could do this. Although we only meet from time to time, I know you are both always with me as I continue my journey here in the physical world.

To my husband, thank you for being a part of my journey. You have taught me many things.

My children, I cannot thank you enough for your understanding of my gift as you both grew up. You both stood so strong and proud in every situation.

To all my pets in my life, especially Krosbee, our golden retriever who taught me so much more about the souls of pets. And to my Chihuahua, Fluffy, who I could confide in when I did not have anyone else. You gave me unconditional love.

Contents

Introduction

Welcome to my crazy—but real—life story as I take you on a journey of what life was like for me growing up. No one in the physical world would believe me and my experiences. I am compelled to tell this story to support and help others through their unique journeys. As you come on this journey with me, you will discover that there is more to life than what we see in the physical world, our loved ones who have passed remain around us and see what we do in our lives, and children like myself may experience a connection to spirits that you will be able to understand and support.

It is about a father-daughter journey lived from two different worlds. In the beginning, it was the excitement of imaginary friends. Eventually, death became a part of my reality. I knew I was different than other children. Many were playing in a world of make-believe. I was not. Trusting and believing in what I knew, felt, saw, or sensed was all I had to rely on.

When I was growing up in the early 1970s, *spirituality* was taboo. Society was not comfortable talking about it. What happens when a young shy girl with a spiritual gift experiences connecting to the other side and faces the challenges of the physical world? It brings joy, hope, and understanding of how fear is conquered. It teaches us how to trust and believe in ourselves.

CHAPTER 1

Who Am I?

At the age of two, I sat on the floor like any other toddler would, playing and talking to many people: three people in general. The only problem with this was that no one else could see them. It became a ritual for me. As my physical extended family came to visit for holidays, it became a game of fun for them to sit around and watch me interact with things they could not see. As time went on, I was teased for having "imaginary friends." I did not understand why they could not see or talk to them. I was asked to describe what I saw. I tried, but they couldn't understand. I sometimes felt scared because it felt different.

Why was I the only one to see them?

I named them and brought them everywhere with me. There were two females and one male. The male, Pelouse, teased me a lot. He would do things, and I would be blamed, but I knew it was him. I had complete conversations with him. At times, I told him what I thought. I did it in a tone that was loud. I would be asked why I was yelling at thin air. He was like a nagging little brother who would pick on his little sister. *Sesame Street* was all the rage for young children at the time; it was my favorite show on TV. Oscar the

Grouch was one of my all-time special connections; he was a green puppet who lived in a trash can.

Many things he met went into his trash can. When Pelouse teased me, I would walk over to our trash can and tell him that I was going to put him in there if he didn't stop pestering me. I was never able to put him in there, but it was humorous for my family to watch. It gave them a chuckle, something to watch to take the nervous edge out of my behavior. It eased a sense of uncertainty regarding those I was really interacting with. They knew it was not from our physical world—but a world they could not see.

Regardless, the three would come with me anywhere I went. As I got older, I spoke more and more freely that they were with me. I even took them on holidays. They became part of my life. It was like having siblings with me. No matter what I was doing or where I was, I looked after them. They looked after me too. I learned to feel comfortable around them. I knew I was a part of them somehow, but I wasn't sure how.

How could I be a part of this group of imaginary friends that no one else could see? It was okay to have my friends who were invisible to others. They were positive and guided me when I wasn't even sure what being guided meant. They protected me. I was safe with them. They understood me, and I understood them. I wished everyone else could just get to know them. They would love them the way I do. My three friends offered unconditional love. Who doesn't want to feel safe and protected? If I could introduce them to my family so that my parents and others could see them, we could all live such a great life together. I wouldn't have to live in two separate worlds.

At that point, my two worlds were too far apart. I knew it. Many people thought I lived in a make-believe world, always looking for excuses for something that could not be easily believed. All children like to dress up and play make-believe, so what made me different? I was always asked a million questions about my imaginary friends, and I was adamant that they were not imaginary. I could see them just like I could see physical human beings.

2

Over time, they became my best friends. I felt so comfortable around them. They would play countless hours with me—from Barbies to swinging on my swing set. Being outside and swinging became a huge part of my life. With every swing through the air, I felt free. I was flying. No one could question me. I was free. Swinging was a normal part of growing up. Relatives wouldn't have to hear me talk about my imaginary friends, although they were swinging right beside me. I spent countless hours on my swings. As a matter of fact, my dad bought me a very special swing set that included monkey bars, two swings, a bar swing, and two hanging circles from which I would flip upside down and hang.

My world that I knew and lived was not make-believe; it was reality. My family owned horses. I had my first horse at the age of six. I felt a huge connection to horses and dogs. The days around the horses were so refreshing. I knew, in some weird way, that they understood me. I felt free around them; it was just as if I was swinging high in the sky. The days I got to go along and feed them were the best days in my life. Life just couldn't get any better than spending time with my dad and the horses.

I was very close to my dad. I was Daddy's little girl. I knew it! Don't get me wrong; both parents loved me very much. It was a long-awaited thirteen years before I came into the physical world. They wanted a child so badly, but they had to wait. You can imagine the excitement my mom felt when she heard the news of her pregnancy. My arrival made headline news in our little town. My dad took me everywhere with him. Our time with the horses was so precious. My dad would not even have to say, "I love you." I looked at him and knew he did—with all his heart. Love radiated from him.

We went to feed our horses, and on one occasion, other people were invited to join the fun. We loaded hay on the back of a pickup truck and drove to the horses. There was only one catch to this joyride: there was not enough room on the back of the truck for my imaginary friends. I asked everyone to move over as I tried to find space to fit them in. I was laughed at and ridiculed for my crazy make-believe behavior, but I was not going anywhere until the people on the truck shifted over and made space. Humorously, everyone shifted around so we could get the show on the road.

I was very shy. I did not like to be noticed or talked to by adults. Maybe it was because adults looked at me differently. From two years old to adulthood, I was described by everyone as being nice. I just wanted to include all children in play. I was liked by adults and children, and I was friendly. I loved everyone and wanted everyone to get along. I believed in sharing. I had the ability to make others laugh—no matter their age. I learned to have a sense of humor.

The first death that affected me was an uncle in 1978. The devastating phone call came, and then my family home turned into a whirlwind. He was an uncle who decided to skip school and take his own life. I had vivid visions of what happened as my family talked about his horrible death. I felt like I had been part of it somehow. I immediately felt how my uncle felt. He was sad and lost. He felt like there was no way out. He was depressed and lonely.

How did I know all of this? My uncle lived on the other side of the country. I did not know him that well. He visited us once. Where was I getting that information? Why was I so drawn into this horrific suicide? I wondered why everyone was so sad. I could not understand it. I knew he was okay. I don't know how I knew, but I knew. Once again, I felt different from other people. I had a different outlook, a different perspective, and I just wanted everyone to understand. I was nine years old and wondered why the adults could not put his death into perspective. Why did no one else feel how desperate he was? Why was it only me?

I knew there was more to life than what is here in the physical world. At times, I felt so frustrated that I could not be understood. I did not realize the long road ahead of me in living this life of feeling all alone. In a sense, it was only the beginning of what was to come.

In September 1979, at the age of ten, my dad walked in the front door when he should have been at work. As I stood in the kitchen beside him, he announced to my mom that my uncle Vic, his brother, had just passed.

It really hurt me to see how this affected my dad. He was the second brother from my dad's large Italian family who had moved on to the other side. I began to feel my dad's grieving emotions. An overwhelming sense that my uncle was okay also came over me at the same time. It was so confusing to me. I could not explain how I knew. I just did.

As more and more family members came to our house to gather strength in each other, more sadness filled the air. It was a negative feeling that I did not like. The air felt thick and heavy with grief. I just wanted to make everyone's pain go away. Why were they acting like that? Uncle Vic was okay. Why didn't they understand it? How did I know he was okay? The sadness filled the air for months. It felt awkward, but I went along with the grieving emotions of my family.

My knowing began to grow, and soon I was feeling energy. My parents' house was a very social house. They had many friends, which went along with an open-door policy. I learned to feel energy from spirits on the other side and the energy of people. I enjoyed some of my parents' friends, but I felt like some were not nice people. I knew when someone was there to take advantage of my dad's kindness. What could I say? How could I voice my feelings? How did I know it? How could I prove it?

The feelings began to grow stronger. I began to have dreams of going places I didn't know. Some repeated themselves every night. I started to have premonitions and feelings of déjà vu. I learned to just be quiet. There were times when I became very afraid of feeling spirit energy. My parents could tell when something had happened or I had experienced something by my screams or body language.

I was on edge all the time. I bit my fingernails down until there was nothing left. I wet the bed longer than anyone should. What was wrong with me? Why would I not wake up in time to go to the bathroom? When I did wake up, why would I not go? I had a bedroom, but I did not sleep in it. There was just too much going on for me. I was never alone. My imaginary friends were there, but many others joined them at different times. I slept in between my parents because I was fearful of the dark. Who would come for a visit in which I did not want to partake? I knew I was somewhat safe below the sheets and between my parents. Many times, my dad had to shower in the morning because of my bed-wetting. It became a joke within our family and close friends. I was a nervous wreck.

I began to feel the energy from TV shows. Some shows frightened me so much that I could not watch them. I felt like I would take on the characters as I watched. If someone hurt a toe, I would feel the pain in my toe. I would take on their feelings. If sadness appeared, I would feel sad.

My mom lived to watch soap operas. Every day at the same time, her favorite show would come on. Even though I would be playing, I could still take on the character's role. Again, I could not understand it. I tried to act normal and live a normal life. I learned to suppress it and not try to make sense of it. How could I make sense of a world that only I knew?

CHAPTER 2

The Day That Changed My Life Forever

On November 28, 1979, at 4:45 p.m., I went figure skating. My dad had lung cancer and was in the city for treatment. I knew he was going back to his hometown later that day. In one way, I wanted to believe he was okay, but I knew he was coming home to die. As I got off the ice, my friend's mom said I could go to their house. My mom would pick me up there. At that moment, something felt wrong. My mom never missed picking me up. I had an overwhelming feeling that my dad was dying. A nervous feeling came over me.

When I was at my friend's house, I could not concentrate. I felt like I was having an out-of-body-experience and felt numb all over. Suddenly, there was a knock at the door. My first thought was my dad had died and they were coming to pick me up. The door opened, and an aunt, an uncle, and my mom were trying to act normal. I saw through it. I was taken to a family member's house. When I walked in, all I could feel was an overwhelming sense of sadness. Everyone was trying to act normal. I was taken into the living room, and I sat on the sofa. My mom told me that my dad had just passed away. I began crying, and other family members came running into the room. I was so confused. I knew my dad was okay. But how? He had just died.

We returned home the next day, and my mom grabbed my dad's jacket, held it tightly, and cried hysterically. At that moment, I grew up. I went from the age of ten to the age of twenty in a short time. I knew I had to look after my mom. She was not going to be able to cope with my dad's death. As company began to arrive, I started to clean the house and be a support for anyone who arrived. I was so confused. I knew my dad passed, but I felt like he was around us and was okay.

I did not understand the viewing at all. I sat next to my mom. I kept staring at his physical body in the casket. I knew it was just a physical body; there was nothing in it. *It* had left. I later found out it was the soul. How did I know it left? Where did it go? I knew—without a physical explanation—that his soul had gone to a place where it was peaceful and not far away. I felt that it had to be where my imaginary friends came from: another world. I had a deep connection to that world and tried to understand to the best of my ability. I had so many questions for my mom, but she could not answer any of them.

As weeks passed, I talked nonstop about my dad to my mom. She was so uncomfortable and sad that she could not even cope with hearing anything I had said. As I went to bed one night, I saw my dad standing next to the bed. When I told my mom, she said, "You're crazy!"

I knew I was not crazy. I could see my dad—just like I could see my imaginary friends. In fact, I believed he joined my friends in that world about which only I knew.

I began to see my dad on a regular basis. I saw him more and more, and I knew he was around me.

My mom buried her head in the sand deeper and deeper.

I began to realize my mom's soul had given up. No matter what I said, she replied, "I give up." She had lost the most amazing man in her life. What was there left to live for? Me. She knew she had to keep going for me. She tried. She did the best she could under the devastating circumstances.

My life soon took an unimaginable turn. Something happened that no one ever could have imagined. My dad stepped in and began raising me from the other side. He kept his commitment as a father; he was there for me in energy form. Many strange, unexplainable things began to happen in my house. It was amazing and confusing at the same time, leaving me in a world to make sense of something that no one else could.

As the stress took over, my mom drank alcohol on a more regular basis. I could feel her pain. Her loss was so huge. I could feel the gaping hole it left in her heart. I watched her for countless hours. From her bed, she would lean over her nightstand and cry into her glass of alcohol on the table. Her pain shone through her actions loud and clear. I felt responsible. How could I ease her pain or make it go away? She was killing herself. I knew she was holding on for me. She longed to be on the other side with my dad, her soul mate. She tried to pick up the pieces to raise me, but at times, she couldn't. Her drinking became an addiction, leading her out of the house. She drank with friends and ended the night at the local bar.

I was left alone in a house that frightened me. I heard strange noises all the time, and I felt the presence of energy or spirits. At the time, I referred to them as ghosts. I could feel my dad beside me—every step of the way. It frightened me to see and sense spirits. I did not know many of them or why they were coming to me. I knew my dad was there to protect me and would not allow them to harm me. My dad made his presence known. I saw him sometimes, but I always felt him next to me.

One night, I called the bar to ask for my mom, which happened over and over. It was after midnight, and I was scared and tired. My bedroom door opened in front of my eyes. I knew it was my dad telling me to go to bed. I had many signs from my dad that gently guided me in the physical world.

I could feel and see my dad standing beside my bed at night.

He was just protecting me. I would see him before I fell asleep. If I ever woke up at night, he was standing there. He never left that spot. I physically missed him so much. I would tell my mom about my experiences at night, but she was not in a place to hear it. She could not make sense of it or understand it. I learned to keep quiet.

In the middle of the ice arena, I felt my dad while I skated. I would be in the center all by myself, ready to begin a solo competition, and knew my dad was right there beside me. I would talk to him in my head while I nervously waited for the music to start.

I learned to make decisions based on the feelings I got from my dad. I followed my gut feeling because I knew he was parenting me. I still had to make my own choices because my soul is here to grow and learn, but I gained confidence in making those choices by knowing he was gently guiding me.

My dad was there for everything. He was still the proud father in the stands. He set boundaries and gave advice. The only difference was that it was coming from the other side: the world about which only I only knew. Many times, I could see him, feel him, or just know he was there. I had a strong emotional bond with him. I could feel him at my big life events: graduations, weddings, and births. I always knew the right path to take or decision to make.

It is hard to explain in physical terms, but a bond was created between the two of us that only I could understand. My imaginary friends were still a huge part of my life, but they grew quieter as my dad began raising me from the other side.

It was a life I began to live with no questions asked. I tried talking to my mom numerous times about it, but she had no response other than I was crazy. I began to live a secret. Who could I tell that my dad was still raising me after he left the physical world? I learned to keep quiet about my imaginary friends, and my secret life began. To outsiders, I looked like a very responsible young woman. Little did they know it was from the advice of my dad. His guidance and reassurance kept me on the path I needed to be on. Many people in my small town asked how I grew up in such a responsible manner.

My mom was never home. As far as anyone knew, I did not have any guidance in my life. I could have turned to drugs or a life of unpredictability. Instead, I grew up making wise decisions and raising my mom.

Growing up was certainly not easy; it was very challenging. I had to be someone I did not want to be. I did not understand how to be. I felt like I was living two separate lives: a human side and a spiritual side.

In my human life, I just tried to fit in so that I appeared to be just like others. I didn't want to appear different from the rest of the kids my age.

In my spiritual life, I knew life was so peaceful and different. The journey continues even after we die in the physical world. We don't die—we just carry on. I know we will all be reunited one day. In the Catholic Church, I saw a painting on the ceiling. That place is so bright, beautiful, and peaceful, and time is not important. It is full of love and kindness. It is so different from the physical world. In the physical world, we judge, put limitations on ourselves, hurt others, and compete to keep up. My two worlds were always in a battle.

Somehow, I managed to get through. I learned to trust and believe in myself when others could not. I knew I was okay. I knew I was supposed to see spirits and connect to the other side. I knew I just had to keep it a secret so that I would not be judged or told I was crazy. Through it all, my dad was right there beside me, ensuring that I was okay. "You can do this for now."

People should feel safe in their own homes, but I didn't always feel relaxed because my mom would catch little glimpses of the life I led. There were times that I could not hide what I was going through. I am sure she could feel my confusion at times. She was my mom, and she wanted to protect me. The problem with my situation was that she couldn't protect me because she did not fully understand it. It was a side about which I had to keep quiet.

Back in the day, people associated every other-worldly connection with witchcraft. I'm sure they thought, *If she sees things we can't, it must be bad.* That thinking was contagious. We live in a negative world. *Let's point out the bad in everything because if something good is going to happen, it will not last for long.* In the physical world, that mentality spreads like wildfire.

How can you convince adults that you are connecting with the other side? There is more to life than what we see in the physical world. Every day was harder and harder as my gift began to grow. I would experience new things all the time. Some days, I did not want to go to school. How could I keep the charade going every day? I would be so stressed that I would physically get sick. I would call it the flu. I had to make excuses for the world in which I existed. I began picking up on other people's feelings and what they were going through. I had my two lives to live, and then I started feeling other people's auras. I did not know how to protect myself from it.

Some days, I would wake up feeling fine, go to school, and be around other people. Suddenly, I would have intense aches and pains. For years, my mom watched the painful process I was going through. She always said, "If it's not your ass, it's your elbow." I couldn't anticipate what malady I would experience next. As I got older and grew even more with my gift, everything from the other side became a part of my life.

Some days, I didn't know if I had a dream, a physic vision, or a mediumship message. I didn't know if I had experienced the event in the physical world. My two worlds merged into an undistinguishable mesh.

In my forties, I woke up one morning with pains in my chest. I felt like I could not breathe. I tried to be brave. Thinking it was heartburn, I made up my usual excuses to cover my real self. I could not handle the pain anymore, and I woke up my daughter and told her. She took me to the hospital, and I was rushed inside. I was told that I was having symptoms of a heart attack. It felt like the doctors and nurses were in panic mode. They were giving me various blood tests and monitoring systems. They gave me an ultrasound. It was such a chaotic situation.

Suddenly, all the symptoms stopped. My tests came back normal;

there were no signs of a heart attack. It baffled the doctors. What was it? Amazingly, after the ordeal, I was fine. It was like a light switched off. Embarrassment overwhelmed me. I was just as puzzled as anyone else, and I was the person going through that confusing chaotic event. How could I suddenly feel fine?

The answer came to me a few years later—after I admitted I was a medium to the world. I learned that an energy, a spirit, can use a medium's physical body to explain how they passed. The answer was simple and understandable to me: it was my grandmother from the other side. She had passed a year before I was born. I didn't know she was one of my imaginary friends. She had taken the opportunity to use my physical body to connect with me because she passed from a heart attack. I had never experienced spirits to that extent. It was new to me. She was just trying to say, "Hi, I am here." My sensitivity to spirits had grown so much. I had to accept that as was part of my life. I always had to ask, "Is it me I'm feeling—or someone else?" I have since learned to distinguish the difference.

After the passing of my father, I became even closer to my grandfather. I grew up with Granddad close to me; he only lived a few blocks away. I spent many days having playdates with him. He would let me put rollers in his two strands of hair. We would have tea parties or play board games. He became a father figure to me. Our relationship continued to grow stronger. I felt that, in some weird way, he understood me.

My mom and I visited him every day. She looked after him because he lived alone. I would help her grocery shop for him and pay his bills. He became such a huge part of my life. Inevitably, he became ill. He was put in the hospital, and then he went into a care home. Later, he was back in the hospital and remained there for years. It was still part of our daily routine to visit him. We would stay until visiting hours were over.

In the middle of the day on December 22, 1983, I could not get him out of my mind. I was thinking about him obsessively. I was out of town doing Christmas shopping with some friends. The only gift I had left to get was for Granddad. Nothing I looked at resonated with me. I wondered why I could not find the perfect gift. He had everything, and he was hard to buy for, but that time felt different. I could not put my finger on the reason. Hesitantly, I decided to buy a ceramic turtle that had special chocolates in its shell. The only reason I got it was because we had to return to our small town, where there were fewer selections. If I didn't buy something then, I wouldn't have anything to give him.

When we returned to our town, I went to my friend's house. Her phone rang, and I knew it was bad news. I could not hear the brief conversation. After my friend's mom hung up the phone, she came over to me.

I looked at her and said, "It's my Granddad, isn't it?"

She teared up and said, "Yes. He passed away today."

I left their house to join my family. I felt like a weight I was carrying had been lifted in some sense. I did not realize I was carrying it until I received the news. As I hugged my mom, so many thoughts went through my head. It was like pieces of a puzzle were coming together. That explained my feelings earlier that day.

I could not make sense of the heavy feeling of knowing. It made sense why I obsessed about Granddad that day. It wasn't about buying the perfect present; it was about knowing he was getting ready to go home to the other side.

He was alone in the hospital when he passed. How could that be? We were always there for him. Why did he go alone? My mom and my aunt could not let that go for years. They carried like a heavy, heartfelt burden. It was something I could not understand. It was so confusing. I knew he was not alone. He was physically alone, but I knew the room was full of spirits, including my grandmother and my dad. They were there to help bring him to the other side. It was the way it was supposed to be. He chose to pass alone. He didn't want any family there to see what he went through before he passed. It was his choice, but the family blamed themselves. I knew Granddad wanted everyone to continue their journeys happily and living their lives to the fullest—and not obsessing over his passing.

CHAPTER 3

Scared of My Own Shadow

I wanted to hide in a bubble. When I followed my mom around the house, she would turn to me and say, "Why are you scared of your own shadow?"

How true, I thought. I was terrified all the time. Everywhere I went and anything I did, I would see, feel, and hear spirit. I constantly witnessed things moving or opening without explanation. I always tried to internally rationalize what was happening around me. I knew I was different from everyone; I felt that. When I tried to confide in my mom, I felt worse. She did not understand. I was told I was crazy.

If we were watching TV in the living room and she got up to go in the kitchen, I stopped what I was doing and ran to step on the back of her heels. I wanted to live in her skin at times. It would help release the fear I had in my own body. I hid behind her legs for pictures. Being teased about my gift, which no one else understood, was just another one of those things that I learned to live with. Being described as shy was an understatement for me.

I always saw unidentified men in the spirit world, and I developed a fear for men in the physical world. The feeling about them in both the spirit and physical world did not sit well with me. For example, my small hometown had just one shoe store, but I would not go if the man who owned the store was working. I did not like the creepy-sounding floor and smell that radiated from that old store. We would wait until the lady was working to buy my shoes. Even the lady's presence did not take away the feelings when I entered that store.

The little, old house I lived in as a child felt haunted. I felt energies in spirit that I could identify, like my dad, and I felt many other spirits as well, which I called ghosts. One spirit man would stand in my bedroom doorway; he was a well-dressed, older man who I knew lived centuries before. Every night, he stood in a black suit, white shirt, and a top hat. I was so frightened that I would put my head under the sheets to make him go away.

I was terrified of walking into the basement. As soon as I got down there, I had an overwhelming feeling of heavy, thick dense energy. I recall one time playing hide-and-go-seek with friends. We turned the lights out to make it scary. I was already terrified, but I went along with the game. I looked up, and I felt like someone was choking me. In the dark, I saw a white noose hanging from the ceiling; the rope was so white it glowed. Why would it glow in the dark? Why did no one else see it? I ran up the stairs and turned on the light. I was done with the game.

I always felt like something was behind me. No matter what I did or where I went, I knew I was not alone. It wasn't just my dad or my three imaginary friends; there were others. I felt like I walked with an entourage. I could feel if someone new came right into my sacred space. I would turn quickly and look because it felt so real. I would double-check to see if it was a human or someone in spirit. I would see them, but sometimes I could sense their presence first. I felt like I was always walking on eggshells. I was worried about seeing something creepy or not of this world whenever I turned around. I constantly wondered if a spirit would try to harm me. Because I lived in constant fear, I would bite my fingernails until they bled. I did not know how to make it all go away. It felt like I was walking through a haunted house at Halloween; it would be scary to begin with, but there would be an ongoing threat of something jumping out to intensify the fear. That was my everyday life in a nutshell.

My father came from an Italian family that had many superstitions. My mom believed in many of the superstitions by which she lived. Some were the usual fun ones: don't walk under a ladder, don't open an umbrella in the house, and don't let a black cat cross your path. Those meant bad luck. However, she also believed in other superstitions that were a little scarier to me. She said if a bird hit your window or a picture fell off the wall, it meant death. Even without her superstitions, I already felt like I lived my life around a scary subject.

I was introduced to one of the superstitions when another uncle passed. I was at a hotel pool with my family and decided to take a shower back in the hotel room. When I was in the shower, I heard a loud bang. It scared me. I grabbed a towel and ran out of the bathroom to investigate. I came to an abrupt halt when I saw that a large picture had fallen off the wall. I was terrified. What caused it to fall? Why did it fall when I was in there alone? Shortly after that event, we received a phone call that an uncle had a massive heart attack and passed. I could not believe it. Was I crazy? It was another thing I could not explain, but we did not talk about it any further. I know it affected my mom, but nothing was said.

My mom owned a plant called a prayer plant. Every time someone died, the plant folded up its leaves. The plant used to scare me half to death. How could my mom believe in the plant and not believe me? I could not grasp my mother's concept of accepting the plant but not understanding me. She had so many superstitious beliefs, but she had a hard time believing what I was experiencing.

I am so thankful for my little Chihuahua mix. I named her Fluffy. The day I got her was the day I gained a new best friend. She could believe and understand me. She didn't think I was crazy. She would look at me with her big, brown eyes, and I knew I was going to be okay. At times, when I needed a friend to listen to me or hear me cry, Fluffy was there. I talked to her constantly. I felt so much support and connection. Fluffy taught me unconditional love. She took away some of the heavy burden, and she was physical company when my mom was not home.

My heart opened, and my love of dogs started. I have never been without a dog since then. They are just a regular part of my life. Dogs have a special place in my heart. I love the special connection and bond I have with them. When I got married, we immediately got a dog. After he was a few years old, I thought we should get another one. The thought would not go away. It played over and over in my head. When I could not take it anymore, I decided to look into the idea. I felt like I was being nagged to get another dog.

I decided I needed a golden retriever. I had to ask myself how I was going to go into a shelter and pick one dog. I knew I would want to bring them all home. I knew I had to try to feed that nagging thought. I went to the dog shelter and explained that I would like to rescue a golden retriever.

The employee at the shelter looked at me and said, "I'm sorry, but we never get golden retrievers in here."

I replied, "Please put my name and phone number down in case you do."

Hesitantly, she wrote down my information.

A week later, I received a phone call. A golden retriever had been brought into the shelter.

I immediately went to the shelter to adopt her. The employees were shocked and could not believe it; the odds were against me. Jenny, like every other golden, was beautiful inside and out. I feel that she came into my life for a reason—just as I was put into her life. She was five years old, and the next five years were the best five years she could have asked for. We went on many outdoor adventures, and she was spoiled. She lived a life of luxury until we found out she had cancer. The vet found a tumor in her stomach. Time went quickly after the diagnosis. It was heartbreaking to have her leave the physical world so quickly. She came into my life so fast, and then she exited the same way. I was fortunate to have spent the time I did with her.

A dog allowed me to feel comfortable. I was not afraid of my own shadow. I knew she felt spirits as well. I felt protected in the physical world in a sense, just like people have guard dogs to protect themselves from other humans. Each dog in my life has come to help me on my journey. They teach me so many amazing things that I can incorporate into my own life.

Another dog I had was a golden retriever that I got as a puppy. His name was Krosbee. The moment I set eyes on him, I knew he was coming home with us. He instantly bonded with our family. Like every golden, he came with his own personality. We nicknamed him the "safety coordinator." He was in our lives to send a strong message of protection.

When my children were young, he would stand guard when they played in the lake. They would try to float out with little surfboards with ropes attached. He would swim out, grab the ropes, and lead them back into shore! It was amazing. Our entire family had such a special bond with him. He was an earth angel in an animal body. He was compelled to help in any way he could. I would sit down and tell him about the obstacles in my life, and he would listen. I knew he understood me.

We had a great five years with him, and then he started to cough. We immediately took him to the vet. After many tests, he was diagnosed with cancer in his lymph nodes. We did everything we could to try to keep him in the physical world, but it was his time to go a couple months after the diagnosis. It was devastating, although I knew he was okay on the other side. He came to me in spirit many times. One day, I heard a male voice. I knew it was coming from Krosbee. I went in for a reality check on myself. *Could this be real? Am I hearing a human voice come from my dog that had passed? Yes! It is real.*

I learned that a soul is a soul. A soul enters a physical human body or an animal body. It has a voice to communicate. Krosbee works alongside my other guides during readings to connect with other animals that have crossed over. He helps them come through in readings for my clients. I feel honored to have him work with me in this way. Communicate with your pets, whether they are here physically or spiritually. You are connecting with them, and they have the capacity to understand you.

I felt exceptionally nervous in hotel rooms. There was so much going on; I always felt busy. I would have anxiety knowing I would have to stay alone. I was scared of my own shadow, knowing a spirit was right there alongside me.

One time, I made a trip to the city. I had to stay in a hotel room by myself. I was awoken abruptly in the middle of the night. I opened my eyes and saw a spirit of a man in a chair at the table. It was dark in the room, but he glowed. He looked like a real human, but he was bright. I was terrified. I reached for the light switch and turned it on as quickly as I could. I wanted to cry, scream, or yell, but I couldn't. I turned on the light, and he still glowed. I saw his black-and-red-checkered jacket. He was an older man, and it looked like he was smoking at the table. I told him to go away, and he eventually did. I felt like he was a spirit that had passed away in that room. I was young and naïve, and I was still trying to figure out spirituality on my own. I never saw him again.

CHAPTER 4

Always Called into Action

After the passing of my dad, I felt like I spent the rest of the time going to funerals. I came from a Catholic family, so they were all Catholic funerals. My oldest aunt kept burying her younger siblings. She would throw herself over the casket before it went in the ground.

I spent countless hours staring up at the beautiful angels on the ceiling of the church. I was so fascinated, and I felt so drawn in at times. I knew there was more than what we had on earth. My imaginary friends were a part of this other world—just like my dad and any others who passed.

I felt like I had some sort of death curse. I loved everyone, and I only wanted happiness for everyone. I often wondered why I was stuck with this curse. What was I doing so wrong to inflict death on my family? I needed to change, but who would I talk to about it? If I stayed quiet, more people would die. If I told my secret, what were they going to do to me? I had never been heard or understood before. Why would they start? All I could do was continue with my life. I hoped it would just stop on its own. I did not understand the chaotic life I was living. It seemed like all my friends lived normal lives. No one died around them. Why did it happen to me? I could not reveal my secret to anyone. I would tell myself that I was living some sort of weird dream. Maybe I would wake up one day and realize all of it was crazy. Day after day, I realized that was not the case. I carried on as usual with the same uncertain feelings, wondering what I would be facing next.

When I heard a family member was sick, I felt compelled to visit. When my dad's brother was in the hospital, I knew I had to go visit. I had to stop what I was doing and go. As I walked through the doorway, the family was gathered around his bed. I knew he was not doing well. He was on his death bed.

The family backed away to make room for my arrival.

My uncle looked at me, pointed to the end of his bed, and said, "There is my brother Willie." He was talking about my dad. He looked back at me, took his last breath, and passed away.

I felt numb. It was like I had gone into shock. I felt like I had taken another victim. I questioned whether I should have visited or not. I replayed the visit over and over in my head. It was like listening to an old record skipping on a turntable.

From that time on, I felt like I was always called to visit when someone was in the hospital. After a while, they jokingly said, "Don't ask Jody to visit you in the hospital because you will die." It confirmed how I felt. I was the curse of death. Did I have some power to make people die? The worst part was that others were noticing the curse I carried.

If there was ever an accident or someone in need, I was always put in that situation to assist. I began to think something was wrong with me. Why did I know things that other family members knew? I knew one of my dad's sisters wanted to die alone with no family present. She hid her diagnosis of lung cancer from the family. It wasn't until she had to be cared for in the hospital that family was alerted. For months, she would cry when I visited her. I felt like something was wrong, but I could not pinpoint it. I was afraid to know because I felt like she would die once her diagnosis became known to me. I tried to ignore the feeling of something being wrong, but I was not surprised to receive a phone call announcing she was in the hospital.

When I arrived, I knew I had to stand in the hallway with the family. I did not feel like going into her room like all the other times. I was there to do a different job: supporting the family members. Everyone took turns going in to say their goodbyes. Her sister was adamant that she was not leaving the room until she passed. Inside, I was screaming, "Let her die the way she wants—alone." How could I let out that voice? How could I tell the family to leave her alone? I was stuck and confused.

Hours went by, and the family became exhausted. Finally, a decision was made to leave, but the stubborn aunt remained. Determination kept her motivated. She was going to be there when her sister passed. I left with a sense of knowing she was going to pass in the later hours of the night, and there was nothing more that I could do.

My aunt was there for hours. When bathroom duty called, she left the room for a moment—and that's when her sister passed. How did I know that? How did I know it was going to unfold that way? None of it made sense to me. Why did she choose to go alone? It was a change for me. It bothered me. I could not understand how this death happened. I could not stop thinking. It haunted me for days. My mind flipped the other way. I started second-guessing. I was always a part of the passing process, which I was not comfortable with. Why was this time different? I did not talk about it because no one understood me. I tried so hard to be normal and act like a person I was not.

I always felt different. I would stand back and watch friends and family interacting. They would laugh, tell jokes, and have conversations. I could not engage. I felt out of place. I had so many thoughts in my head that I could not think straight enough to stay focused and carry on a conversation.

My dad's side of the family kept passing away. Maybe I had a curse on his side. How could it be? As the months went by, my feelings were validated. I had many other experiences as they kept passing. It was a large Italian family, and I knew I had my work cut out for me. The work was confusing, and I did not enjoy it. I did not understand.

I knew my dad was guiding me in every step of my life. I knew to trust him; it was some sort of purpose for me. With his warm, gentle soul beside me, I kept going. Living in a physical world of confusion, I woke up every day in his presence. I went to bed every night with him beside my bed. I went along with what I had been dealt. I missed him terribly. I wouldn't question that. How could I miss him when he was with me? It was tough. I would hear his favorite country music artist and cry. I was so confused. I only had him to turn to. He understood me. I would pick up the pieces of my breakdown. I knew I had to continue with him by my side.

As time went on, more of his family passed. That was when animals started to come into my life. The physical animals gave me signs, and I listened to them. I loved eagles, and I was afraid of owls. Eagles appeared more and more frequently in my life and brought messages with them.

When I was in my twenties, I saw an eagle on one of my favorite beaches. It brought joy to me at first glance. It did not take long for me to realize that it wasn't circling above my head. It flew in a straight line to capture my attention. It turned around and flew back again. It was different than what I had already experienced. What was it trying to say to me? I knew there was something. It was a new part of the language I did not understand. I asked a question in my head and felt a chill. It was a hot summer day. *What is this all about?*

I soon learned that another aunt on my dad's side had passed away. That experience taught me that I was growing with the curse. The animals were getting involved, and I realized the eagle had sent me a message. From that moment on, I began to watch for messages from physical animals.

CHAPTER 5

Growing up Confused

Everyone has dreams, right? That's what I thought. Mine were a little different. The dreams I had were so vivid and so real. My dreams consisted of three categories.

One category consisted of the dreams where I was meeting my loved ones who had passed. It felt so real. It was like I was hugging them or having a conversation with them. The second category of dreams consisted of getting messages through symbols. As I got older, I would refer to a dream symbol guide book.

The third way that I dreamed was of spirit animals. Each animal has its own message and meaning. I had one animal totem that I did not appreciate seeing because, when I did, someone in my family died.

The first category was the one I favored the most. I was going to a space that belonged to the world I had brief encounters with so many times. It was the place my imaginary friends came from, a place of happiness and freedom and no judgment. There, I could feel like I was physically hugging my dad. I woke up crying so many times when I had dreams about my dad. It was so real. It felt like I had really had an encounter with him. We always met in the same place. The sidewalk next to my favorite swing set was a sacred place for me.

It was a place that understood me. I would walk along the sidewalk until I met him. I looked forward to meeting him and hugging him. He hugged me back so tightly. I knew our meeting time was brief. Why? Why? Why? It was so brief. I missed him so much.

I would say, "Dad, you need to stay longer."

His reply was the same every time: "I have to go."

It felt like such a short time with him. I learned that our brief meetings were due to the energy connection. It could only last so long. After waking up and realizing I had an encounter with him on a different level, I felt like I had been given a renewal of life. I felt recharged. The feeling was different. I still knew he was beside me, protecting and guiding me, but the meetings were different. I longed for them.

The second category of spiritual dreams involved symbols. I learned the difference between regular dreaming, which consisted of things on my mind that day, and being guided through symbols. I had a reoccurring dream about water for many years. The dream began with jumping into a swimming pool. It was three feet deep at the edge. I would jump in and find that there was no bottom. I would keep sinking until I woke up in pure panic, gasping for air. I knew there was a message, but I didn't know what it was.

At the same time, I was faced with another reoccurring dream about bubble gum. My mouth was so full of bubble gum that I could not chew, swallow, talk, or breathe. I tried to talk, yell, scream, or get something out. The harder I tried, the more my mouth filled with gum. I would wake up gasping for air. What did this dream mean? Fear went through my mind. What if I couldn't wake up next time? What if it took my voice away? Who would hear me? I woke up every time, but I was more confused than ever.

I later discovered that all the spiritual dreams were guiding me. They showed the state of mind I was in. They described who I was and what I was going through. In my early adult years, I learned to accept things. I didn't question them in depth. I went through a big change. I started to discover who I really was. As I hit an all-time low, a bottom in my life, my dreams began to change.

The water dream took on a different focus. When I jumped in, I touched the bottom of the pool, gained strength, and pushed myself up to the surface. I got air and began to breathe. I found the strength deep inside and believed I could push off with my toes to gain momentum and get that breath of life. It was a groundbreaking moment to get that breath of life. From that point on, it all went uphill. The bubble gum dream disappeared when I learned to speak up for myself, gain confidence, and voice who I was. I did not have to hide anymore. I knew who I was and what I wanted. It was a time of acceptance for me. I was happy with who I was, and I was okay with the skin I lived in. I did not want to pretend anymore. I couldn't do it.

Prior to the dream of acceptance, I spent countless hours, days, and months visiting doctors and specialists. I felt like I was falling apart. Was I starting to fall to pieces? I needed answers, but I couldn't find them. I continued my life of secrecy.

The third category of dreams involved spirit animals. If I dreamed of a certain animal, I knew there was a message for me. I would have a vision of an animal in my dream. When I woke up, I looked up the meaning of the animal. I needed to see what the meaning of that animal was.

Why was I being guided by animal spirits? I felt like so many other confusing things were already guiding me. How did the animals fit into it all? I became fearful of the owl. The fear became so horrifying that I did not want to fall asleep. It had a meaning of its own. It affirmed that I had a curse of death. It let it be known loud and clear that it was my partner in crime. The owl knew about death. It took it upon itself to warn me when someone was going to die. Why? I was having a difficult time and was living in total confusion. Why was the owl confusing me about death?

In my dreams, the owl brought certain looks that only I understood. If the owl looked me straight in the eye, I knew someone close to me was going to pass. The owl looked at me one night, and the next day, my uncle passed away in front of me at the hospital.

If the owl came in a dream and gave me a sideways look, I knew something bad was going to happen. Someone would get sick, but they would not die.

I feared owls. If I encountered an owl on the cover of a magazine or book or on jewelry, pillows, blankets or TV shows, I was terrified. *Why does it keep following me? Why can't this beast of death leave me alone?* I didn't know where to turn. I was deathly afraid of owls.

As I grew in spirituality, I learned that animal spirits came to me in the day to bring me messages. Many birds fly around every day, but when one particular bird sits on a tree outside my house, making so much noise to get my attention, I know there is a message to pay attention to. If I am driving down a dirt road and a squirrel runs out in front of me, it is a sign. A gut feeling tells me so.

My mom got pneumonia and was put in the hospital. I happened to be driving on the highway later that day and noticed an owl on top of a telephone poll. I looked up, and we locked eyes. It turned its head halfway and looked the other way. I immediately knew my mom was not going to pull out of it. She passed a couple of months later.

I learned to completely trust my dreams and the physical messages that the animals brought to me. I needed to hear the messages. I had to trust and believe they were keeping me on the right path.

As I dove farther into spirituality by fully accepting who I am, I learned that the owl is my friend and not enemy as I once believed. The owl is one of my spirit totems. The owl works with me—and always has. The owl is a messenger. He can deliver any type of message. I have learned to trust and believe in the owl. He is with me for my highest good. We are not death partners in crime. We work together to bring love and light into the world. I am fortunate to have such a powerful and beautiful animal working alongside me.

I listen to the voices of the spirit animals. They have so much to tell us, and they can guide us. They can answer our questions and keep us on the right path when we ask questions.

CHAPTER 6

Knowing and Admitting

At the age of twenty, I had another spiritual awakening. I became extremely sensitive to energies. I began to have many different experiences with spirit.

I finally admitted to myself that my gift was getting stronger; I was growing and becoming aware of what spirituality meant to me. I allowed myself to understand it a little more. It was a time when John Edward, a psychic medium, came out with the television show called *Crossing Over*. He did live studio readings with people who were in the audience.

Rosemary Altea, another medium and healer, was appearing on talk shows. *The Eagle and the Rose* explained her experiences with spirit. It was a breakthrough moment for me. I felt at home and normal. It confirmed that I was not crazy. I started to finally feel excitement about my gift, and it slowly washed away some of the fear. *You Own the Power* supported the practice in working with energy and allowed me to dive deeper into the subject. It contained exercises to practice with energy. I became even stronger at using energy source with practice; I grew stronger in my spiritual mediumship abilities. My palm centers became so hot, and the energy was released to flow. There was no denying that it was a gift, but I did not know what to do with it. I started speaking about it more freely with my boyfriend, and he is now my husband. He believed me, and when he didn't understand, he knew to nod his head and follow along.

I grew stronger with every exercise I practiced. I knew that I had to reach out to the experts for help. Writing letters was the best form of communication at that time. It took courage, and I had dig deep to retrieve it. Fear was trying to hold me back. The what-ifs started to emerge. What if she thinks I am crazy like everyone else? What if I am truly different than everyone—even her? After an agonizing few weeks, I wrote the letter and put it in the mail. I tried to wait patiently for a response. With every day that passed, I hoped I would receive a response that she could be a support for me in some way. I needed it at that time in my life. The energy with spirits had been building, and I did not know what to do with it. When the letter arrived, it was a form letter stating that she was a very busy person, but thanks for the letter. I was devastated. Why another block? If I was meant to do the work, why was I encountering so many roadblocks? As usual, I continued on. What else could I do? It was definitely part of a learning curve.

I kept quiet about who I was to the rest of my world. Friends had no idea of my true identity. When I felt spirits around them of their loved ones who had passed, I would awkwardly and gently add little comments into our conversation. I learned to do it while keeping my gift quiet. I would add pieces of my knowing from messages I was receiving, but I would make it seem like they had already given me the information.

I was learning to juggle both worlds at the same time. It was too soon to reveal my reality and who I was. I was getting a little more comfortable with myself and gaining confidence. My dad walked every step with me. I felt the urge to learn more about this gift. I was always asking, "If I am supposed to work as a medium, how, when, and where do I get started?" That question haunted me for another twenty-four years.

My dad always had to remind me to be patient. Patience is definitely not a strong part of my human personality. It is something that I have to be aware of and conscious of. I work hard to find a balance on my patience level. All I could trust and believe was that my dad was right there beside me and taking every step with me. I knew I had to wait. I was learning to trust and believe in him and his guidance when I wanted something. I knew that I could do it because he only wanted the best for me. I learned to let go of things I had no control of.

I encountered new spiritual experiences in my life. I was learning and growing. With every death I encountered, I learned something new. I was not as scared anymore. The fear started to diminish as I realized that I was not the curse of death. It was part of my gift to help people cross over to the other side. Just when I thought I had death figured out, another situation appeared that made me question it.

My cousin Barry was like a brother to me. We had an opportunity to hang out one weekend when we were in our early twenties. We decided to go on a road trip. On the drive into Fernie, the small town where I grew up, we had a talk like we had never had before. We had a heart-to-heart talk about his life. He talked about his life, what he had gone through, and what he was going through. He had taken steps to improve his life. Someone we both knew had been in a car accident. He explained he would expect from family and friends if he was ever in a car accident like that—where he was killed but the driver lived. The talk sent shivers down my spine. It was a talk like we had never had before. It felt dark and scary, but I knew I had to listen. I didn't question it.

We visited many family members that weekend. On Sunday, we returned home. I dropped him off and said goodbye. I vividly remember him jumping over the fence and into his yard. It was so strange. As he jumped the fence, my vision went into slow motion. I blamed it on being tired from the busy weekend. I still found excuses for myself on a daily basis. As I pulled away, I felt off and sad, but

I didn't understand why. The answer came to me with a middle-of-the-night call from my mom a few nights later. Barry had been killed in a car accident with the exact scenario he had spoken about.

At first, the news took me by surprise, but I quickly came to remember what I had experienced before the call came in. I was sound asleep, but I had a visitation from Barry. He said goodbye. As the words rang through my head in my dream, I jumped up in a startled manner. I looked around and felt his soul leaving my room. It was like a wind blowing through an open window. I was frozen with fear. What had happened? I had never experienced something like that before, and I had seen some strange situations unfold. When I was able to fall back asleep, the phone call came in.

After a few days of trying to put the pieces of that situation together, I had the feeling that his soul knew that his life in the physical world was about to end. Years later, Barry validated my thoughts in a reading.

The most common theme in this book is that I knew or had a knowing. Growing up, I could feel, see, and sense spirit, and I always had a knowing. I am not talking about worldwide predictions. I knew what was going to happen in some instances. I grew up thinking it was normal and that they were just thoughts in my head. I would know before people dropped by, when someone feeling sick or sad, who was calling on the phone, or if someone was going to cancel plans. It was always a heavy feeling. I would be consumed with a feeling of separation from myself. I had to learn how to decipher my own personal thoughts and the spirit messages.

I did not leave my house much. I preferred having people over to my safe place. I would pick up on so much energy at other people's houses. It was confusing and frustrating for me. When I was younger, if I did stop in at a friend's house for a few minutes or meet the parents, I instantly knew who they were. I knew if they were sincere and genuine, if they put up a facade, or if they were different from who they pretended to be. I always knew if someone had an ulterior motive. I learned from my human emotions to always give people a second chance. By allowing myself to do this and incorporating it into my life, I put myself out there to be hurt and used many times. I knew to go with my first gut feeling, but always gave people the benefit of the doubt. We are always given choices in life.

I would tell myself they would change. After being hurt and used for many years, I began to trust my first gut feeling about someone when I meet them. It is about trusting and believing in the feelings and messages I receive at a particular moment. I need to work with the message I get. I have also realized that I cannot change other people.

It has taken many years, but I have finally come to the conclusion that every human in the physical world is given choices. Everyone has to be responsible for the choices they make in their lives. Other individuals cannot make those choices for them. If we try to, we are not allowing that individual's soul to grow while we are here in school.

We come to earth so our souls can learn and grow. Some of the hardest obstacles are our greatest teachers. The hardest times and the roughest patches can hold the biggest lessons we have to learn. If patterns are repeated, we better look hard and admit our mistakes so that they are not repeated. If repetition occurs, you have missed an important part of the lesson you need to learn and grow. You need to reevaluate and make a different choice. Listen to your intuition; it is your greatest teacher.

CHAPTER 7

Raising My Family: The Secret Circle

At the age of twenty-six I had a daughter. Two years later, I had a son. As I raised my children, I incorporated my spiritual beliefs into their lives. I talked about my father, their grandfather. I let them know Papa had passed, but he was still there for me—and for them. I assured them that it was okay to talk to him and other loved ones who had passed. I explained that I was different in that I had a gift. I could communicate with those who had passed away and crossed over. I was open and honest, and I openly shared every aspect of my life. Overall, it was our family secret. I shared stories of what my life was like growing up and how afraid I was at times. I told them how I lived knowing there was more, and at times, my two worlds collided. As I grew spiritually, my family did as well. I was open and honest with every move I made and every thought I had. I made choices and decisions based on my spiritual gifts and the messages I received. We lived happily in a four-bedroom home in a quiet cul-de-sac. The area was safe, and the neighborhood children could play safely on the street.

Both of my children are spiritually gifted. They are each unique, but at the same time, they are similar. My daughter is very strong, loud, and ready to take on the world. She is a go-getter and an overachiever. No matter what situation she is in, she is compelled to help. I noticed this behavior when she started interacting and playing with friends. She was friendly, wanted to share, and made sure everyone got along. She had trouble sleeping from day one. I knew she was afraid to be in her bedroom at nighttime. She would look for any excuse not to go to bed. When I would finally get her to sleep, she would wake up screaming hysterically. She was always looking around the room with fear in her eyes. Once she was safe in my arms, she would calm down—but she did not want to go back to bed in her bedroom. In those moments, I knew she was connecting with spirit. She is an earth angel, and beautiful white light surrounds her aura.

Spirits knew they could contact her. I was afraid. I did not want my child to grow up the way I did, being afraid of everything. At that point, I made a conscious decision to make sure I supported her in any way I could for the rest of her life. I knew she was protected. If she pointed at the wall and no one was there, I would ask, "Who do you see?"

She would just smile and giggle. I would say, "Do you see your papa?"

Encouragement and support are key elements when you have a spiritually gifted child. As time went on, I knew she could feel energy. If we went somewhere, she would say, "I don't like it in here." She would talk about situations as if she had already lived them.

I thought, *You are too young to know that stuff.*

Whatever the situation, I supported her. She was very sensitive and could pick up on other children's energies. If someone was having a bad day, she would feel bad too. At the age of four, she began to get migraine headaches. We saw many doctors, but nothing helped ease the extreme pain, nausea, and vomiting. It was spirits trying to connect. The really bad headaches seemed to happen when she was overwhelmed or if there was too much going on. If she went to a birthday party or a community event, the spirits did not leave her alone. She became stimulated very quickly. I could not take her anywhere in the early part of the evening because she could not sleep and would get a migraine. Because spirits were always trying to connect with her, she had trouble with physical people in her space for too long. She felt overwhelmed and claustrophobic. She was young and did not understand. I monitored things for her. She also became an animal lover, especially dogs. She would play with our dogs for hours. One dog, Dino, who she knew from birth, passed in my arms with all of the family gathered around in 2009. She immediately understood death in the physical world.

In 2013, my daughter was exposed to two deaths: Grandma and Krosbee. She knew she had to be there for Grandma and bravely stood beside her bed until she passed. She talked to her and said loving messages—even though she knew Grandma looked like she could not physically understand. My daughter knew what to do, and I knew to let her do what she felt was right. I was not afraid. I knew she could handle it. It was part of her journey in the physical world. She also has the ability to help people pass and cross over. It felt so good to support her by letting her know she was not crazy. She could embrace her gift.

A few months later, her dog died. She sat beside him and supported him as he crossed over. She still feels him around her. Krosbee's big bushy tail never stops hitting her in the back of the knees. Many times, she turns around to look at something, but—to the physical eye—nothing is there. Krosbee leaves her many signs to tell her he is okay.

My daughter has been pulled toward health care. She is working on her degree in registered nursing and hopes to keep moving forward in the field. The spirits have guided her to work in that area, and she is guided toward certain situations at certain times. She is spiritually gifted and has learned to follow, trust, and believe in her intuition. She finds herself in many coincidental circumstances. She is working for spirit—just as I do—in a discrete way.

It brings comfort to know that I can support her with her spiritual gift. We are connected on a deeper level. We have a special bond; it is a soul mate bond. Living hours away from each other, we feel each other's emotions. I can feel her headache or stress, and she can feel mine. Sometimes, my situation shows up in her dreams.

My son was born twenty-two months after my daughter. He entered the world with a calm, grounded, and relaxed attitude. He has patience and takes the time to get things done right. He is an old soul, and he has been on earth many times before. He is knowledgeable in areas that do not match his physical age. He is an earth angel and feels compelled to help people. He finds himself in situations where he can be of assistance.

When he was learning to talk, he yelled, "Papa's here!"

I was taken aback for a second. I said, "What does he look like?" I was curious about how well he could see spirits. He described my dad perfectly. I was so excited. He was happy and ready to play with him. At that moment, I knew I had another gifted child. As he grew up, I supported him just as I did my daughter. If anything came up that was questionable, we would talk about it.

My husband continues to be a big support in my life. I met him when I was sixteen years old. He knew from our first date that I had a gift—and he didn't question what he saw me experience. We drove down a dirt road, which is something that all the teenagers did in our small town. It was starting to get dark. He pulled over to the side of the road, and I screamed. I saw two spirits: one male and one female. They crossed the road, right in front of the truck, and then they vanished. I was frantic. My reaction gave my secret away. How was I going to explain it to someone I hardly knew? Panic set in, but I was honest with him. I said, "Oh my goodness. Did you see those two people crossing in front of us?"

He laughed, opened the door, and got out.

I started to sweat. I felt hot and nervous, and I didn't know what to do. *He thinks I am crazy just like everyone else.* I beat myself up for a few minutes.

37

He got back in the truck, looked at me, and said, "I think it was exhaust you saw." He said it with a little smirk, but it was good enough for me. We continued to date, and we went on to get married. We still laugh about our first date.

We raised our children from birth to the ages of seven and nine in the same house on the cul-de-sac. The house sometimes had unwanted guests. Spirits I did not know would contact me at different times. I was not comfortable in the basement of that house. Toys would start going off when I walked down there to get something. It was a cold, unsettled energy.

When two female spirits came to me in a dream, I asked them what they wanted. All of a sudden, I heard a bag of toys falling over downstairs. It really scared me. I knew I had gifted children, and I did not want them to be bothered by unfriendly spirits. I felt like it was time to get out.

I had many nights when I could not sleep. One night, I kept getting a repeated message through a dream. The message was that we had to sell our house and build on the piece of property we owned. How could I tell my husband that it was the right time to build? Well, I did. I knew we had to look into building. If we started then, the building process would flow. After a few more sleepless nights, I decided to do something about the message.

While I was in a deep sleep one night, I was awakened by a loud air horn going off in my ear. I jumped up and wondered who was blowing an air horn in my ear. I looked around and didn't find anybody. I took a moment to clear my thoughts and realized it was a very important message. I had to pay attention to it. More memories of the dream came into my head. It was like putting a puzzle together. It became obvious that it was time. If we didn't take the opportunity, we could go down the wrong path. I knew I had to get things moving. I made an appointment to meet with a builder, and my husband was reluctant to go. He came along just to see why I was so persistent and adamant about building. We soon found out that building prices had gone down a little. We immediately found a plan that we both liked. Things started to flow smoothly. How could it be? To my knowledge, life was not always easy or flowing in a calm manner. The decision was made. We would build if our house sold. We bought a for sale sign to try to sell it ourselves. We stapled it on the deck and waited to see what happened.

A few days later, a friend of mine told another friend about our decision. She came to look at the place, and she said, "I will think about it." As she was pulling out of the driveway, the sign fell off the deck! I giggled inside. I knew she liked it, and I knew she would buy it.

A few days later, the phone rang with an offer. The house sold! It was divine timing, which is about listening and understanding how we are guided. For some reason, it was time for us to move on.

I have encountered so many similar experiences in my life. I was constantly guided in what to do for my children. I openly shared all experiences that I would go through and messages I would receive. It was frustrating for them at times, but they accepted my craziness! As a family, we shared many funny jokes about my abilities. It just made our situation more comfortable and bearable. Our house had an open-door policy, and they had many friends over to play or hang out, but we still kept our secret quiet.

CHAPTER 8

I Am a Medium

I finally decided to come out of the spiritual closet in June 2013. A tragic event in our community led me to the decision.

After the high school graduation ceremony, I received a phone call. There had been an accident in our community. I was asked if I knew a young man named Daniel. Immediately, I knew it was my friend's nephew.

I picked up the phone and made the call that no one ever wants to make. Janet answered in tears. She confirmed that Daniel had been killed in the accident.

I gathered my belongings and some food and headed over to Daniels's mom's house. It was a hot summer day, and family and friends had gathered outside. I could see the devastation in their eyes. I wanted to stand up and yell, "But Daniel is okay. He is here!" I knew I couldn't. I struggled in my own head. I kept looking over at his mom and feeling her pain. She was crying about her son. I could not bear to see it anymore. I knew Daniel was there. I argued, felt sick, and wondered what to do with my own thoughts. I felt the sadness and devastation from everyone there. I wanted to take their pain away. I wanted them to understand how I felt, but I couldn't say anything. I was living in a facade. How could I speak up at a time like that? My whole life kept flashing before my eyes. I felt the intensity of my thoughts. I felt like I was hitting rock bottom. *Where am I going from there? I am an honest person. Why can't I just be honest about who I am? What if I tell them I can connect with Daniel and tell everyone that he is okay? How will they respond?* The choice I made was not an easy one, but as usual, I opted to leave.

For months after Daniel's death, I met with his aunt for lunch or coffee. I tried to help Janet work on her grief resulting, and it changed my life forever.

We met at a restaurant for lunch, and our conversation started out as normal.

Suddenly, she said, "My sister believes in all this weird stuff … like Daniel is leaving her signs that he is okay."

We locked eyes, and she asked what I thought about that *stuff.*

I choked on my pasta and told her what I thought. Three hours later, I was done explaining my life story, including the details of who I really was.

She told me that I needed to do something about my amazing gift because I would be able to help so many people.

I do not remember the drive home. I beat myself up and thought, *Why did I let the cat out of the bag? It was my secret.* I thought I had lost my best friend. I didn't think she would call me again because she must have thought I was crazy.

Fortunately, Janet called me the next day. I was so excited. She was so supportive. For weeks, we continued to meet on a regular basis. Each time, I would update her on the progress I was making. I enjoyed meeting with my friend; she understood me. It was like a new chapter of my life had begun. The more I talked about who I really was, the faster I grew. I felt empowered. I was revealing who I really was, and my friend was encouraging me to keep going. Every time we met, I gave her little readings; the messages were coming through. It shocked me just as much as it shocked her. The messages were so validating and true. She knew Daniel was okay on the other side.

One night, we met at a coffee shop. As we sat down, I kept getting a vision in my mind from Daniel. I knew he wanted to connect with her. I asked him what the message was. He wanted to talk about my friend's son. I looked at her, and she knew what I was going to say. She began to see the look I get when I connect with the other side. I asked if it was okay to give her a message from Daniel.

She definitely wanted to hear more from Daniel!

I began, and Daniel talked about her son. I asked if her son was doing something in mud.

She said, "Well, I think he is at home."

I said, "Well, Daniel is saying something about him being in mud."

She called her daughter and asked if everything was okay. She said her brother was not home. He was out somewhere. She hung up the phone.

A few minutes later, a call came in. She screamed, and the look on her face was priceless. She jumped up and ran around the coffee shop. She yelled, "Oh my goodness. You are not going to believe this!"

All I could do was laugh. I knew it had to be some sort of validation—and it was. Her son was with some friends, and his vehicle was stuck in the mud. It had just happened, and Daniel was there to let his aunt know! I believe it was planned. I don't believe in coincidence. It was planned to teach us that—no matter what time of day or where you are—our loved ones see what we are doing!

I learned something every time I met with her. I believe Daniel has more work to do from the other side. He works with me. I did not know him physically in this world, but his family and friends always spoke so highly of him. He was a well-respected young man. As time went on, I practiced with friends in the evenings and on weekends since I still had a full-time job as a social worker.

Janet invited me to her house to visit with her relatives one evening. As I started getting ready to go, Daniel appeared. I asked if he wanted me to give them a message. He definitely wanted to give a message to his family.

I was new at giving messages, and I was still learning what to do on a daily basis. It was a new situation, but I made a deal with him. I said, "Let me get ready. Once I get there, I will ask if I can give a message from you."

As I started driving, I could feel my mind entering the other world. I had kept my connection to that other world a secret for so long. I knew that was the world I would connect to in order to receive and deliver messages. That world is known as the other side. It is where we cross over when we pass. That world is not that far away. It is right here—all around us. We have to be open to it to understand and receive signs from it.

I missed the turn, but I turned around and eventually made it to her house. As we gathered around to visit, I knew Daniel was there. He could not wait to send some messages. I found my physical mind going back to the other side. I could not think or concentrate on the conversation. I could not take that feeling anymore. I just had to say it. It was a challenge for me, but I knew I had to say it. I could not walk away this time like all the other times in my life. I was getting hot with energy, and my hands were pulsing and sweating. I felt like I was going to blow up.

I said, "I can't concentrate anymore. Daniel is here and would like me to relay a message. Is that okay?"

Everyone agreed.

As I started relaying the messages, I was just as shocked as they were. I could not believe how I just started relaying the messages. It came so naturally, and I felt so comfortable. I knew that was what I needed to be doing. It felt so right. The best part was that I was sharing the other world with people who really appreciated it. My heart began to open more and more.

As the validating messages came in, they were shocked. They asked if they could invite others over to witness the reading. In the end, seven people gathered around to hear wonderful healing and validating messages from Daniel. Daniel made it loud and clear that he was okay on the other side. He proved that he did not miss a beat. He saw what was going on in the physical world on a daily basis.

It did not erase the pain of his passing, but it brought everyone to ease that he would always be a huge part of their lives—even from the other side. It brought some healing to them to know he was with all of them.

It boosted my confidence to relay the beautiful healing messages from Daniel to seven people. I felt like the crazy life I had led to get to that point was suddenly worth it. *If this is what I am supposed to do, I would not trade the experience I went through.*

My name began to spread around our little town. I made business cards, a website, and social media profiles. I was out there for the world to see—more prepared than ever to assist in helping. I always ask myself, "In what way can I bring healing to someone?"

It is so sad to I watch people carry the pain and burden of losing a loved one. I immediately want to step in and alleviate their pain. I began to build a clientele, and as I was getting ready to go to a different group reading, Daniel appeared.

I said, "Oh, no. Daniel, I am not going to give a reading to your family. It is a different group." I am always learning in this work, but what happened next was a memorable honor. Daniel told me that he wanted to work with me. He was going to be one of my many guides—like my dad. I could not believe what I was being told. I attended the group reading, and Daniel was there to help me. He still works with me.

It was a planned event in my life. I admitted my truth to my friend after Daniel passed. Why did I tell that particular friend? I had lived in two worlds for so long without anyone knowing. Why was it time to tell her? After my announcement, my life completely changed. Daniel became one of my guides. It is all in the power of the universe.

I felt empowered and knew I had to step out of the closet once and for all. I had been carrying my burden by living two separate lives for too long. I finally announced my identity to the world! I have been learning and growing from that moment on. It feels wonderful to know that I can communicate with those who have crossed over. I can help so many people heal in the physical world. I love what I do!

Subsequently, I started my mediumship business. The feedback from my clients has been overwhelmingly positive; they feel a sense of closure and amazement. Every reading I do is different. Each one has its own validation that the messages are coming from their loved ones in spirit. They share stories only they would know happened. In one reading, a mom who had passed talked about a particular song and opening a box. The day before the reading, my client had been in a store and picked up a jewelry box that was playing the song I had described. It was strong validation that her mom was with her in that store at that time.

The readings can also bring in apologies, which allow the person who is left here in the physical world to begin healing and carrying on with their journey in a happy, healthy, positive way. Loved ones from the other side can apologize if it is needed. They have a life review after they cross over and discover how their soul grew in the physical world. They learn who they may have harmed or helped.

I received calls about ghosts residing in houses. I went to the houses to investigate, and it was loved ones from the other side leaving signs that they are okay.

A mom who was worried about her son called me. He had talked about a man playing with him and touching his hand. He was terrified.

On my way to the house, a man appeared in my vehicle. I instantly felt chest pains. It was like he had passed from a heart attack. He referred to himself as "Dad." The feelings became more intense as I walked into the house. The house energy felt calming and peaceful; I knew a family member was trying to connect. The gentleman in spirit—the one who drove over with me—was there. As I connected with him, he gave me validating evidence that I could relay to the family. I explained what happened on the drive over and what he had to share. The outcome of the story was that her son was spiritually gifted, and he had the ability to connect with his grandfather. The grandfather was the contact from the other side. It was his dad's father. He wanted to say he was okay. It brought comfort, healing, and closure to the family. I gave the mom ideas for how to make sure her son was spiritually protected. After the experience, he began to sleep better. He was not afraid anymore. The support of his family was so positive, and it will continue to be so.

My experiences teach me so much about the other side. A month ago, I had an experience that was new to me. Two days before Christmas, I decided on a whim to visit a second cousin. She was thirty-nine years old and had stricken with progressive multiple sclerosis. She was in a care home.

When I am meant to be somewhere or do something in my life, I am guided there. I drove to another town to pick up a family member in a snowstorm. It was Christmastime when I decided to pursue my adventure. As I was driving by the care home, I knew I had to stop. For a second, I wondered why. I wanted to get home and out of the snowstorm. I heard her name, and I found myself pulling into the parking lot.

As I walked into her room, I could not believe what I saw. She was sleeping in a bed, but I also saw her soul standing beside the bed. I was shocked at first. I had never witnessed something like that. I felt calm and at peace. I communicated with her through thought. She looked happy. She was free from her physical body for a moment. It was nice to see because she suffered physically. Every time I talked to her, her body twitched. Her soul was so happy and at peace. She looked healthy, and she had color in her face. Her physical body showed the suffering that it had been enduring for years. She was able to stand, and she was out of her wheelchair. She was communicating. She could not communicate in the physical world.

We had a great conversation, but I needed to get back on the highway. I said my goodbyes and left. Two days later, on Christmas,

I got the call that she had passed. My first reaction was shock, but the story of what I had witnessed started to unfold. I had witnessed her soul leaving the physical body. She was just waiting for her physical body to shut down. I did not realize it at the time because I have a boundary set that I do not want to know when people are going to pass. I was so thankful that I had that time with her and that she allowed me to witness that event of her passing. I realized why I was guided to visit her.

After hiding my spiritual side for decades, I am so relieved that I can put my gift to good use. However, it isn't free of lingering consequences. My family has seen me battle with constant distractions and spirits visiting me and talking to me. My daily routine can be interrupted by thoughts or messages. I rarely have alone time. I might see or hear something that will lead me to tangential thoughts or emotions that create anxiety. When I have a headache, I have to ask, "Is this spirit-related pain or my own physical pain?" I have learned to set strong boundaries so I can go out in public, but the boundaries do not always work.

A few months after I came out of the closet, I found myself being thrown into a brand-new experience. I walked into the living room, and my daughter looked at me and said, "Did you hear about that missing boy?"

All of a sudden, without realizing it, I described the entire detailed scenario of what had happened.

She told me the story had not been released. The media was reporting that a young boy was missing, and that was it.

I suddenly felt sick. I started to shake. I knew that I was getting psychic visions of what happened. What was I going to do? I wanted to help, but who could I tell? With the help of family and friends, I decided I needed to report the information to Crime Stoppers. I told them who I was and what was happening in the visions. The visions carried on for months. My life became consumed with what had happened. I called and asked to speak with investigators because the anxiety I was getting from the case was starting to consume my life. I felt like I was losing my entire summer. I did not get to speak to the investigators, but I found out that a key piece of evidence was important and had helped find the person who was involved in the case. I knew I had to learn how to do protection work so that not every murder or mystery case would bother me. I will be learning more and embracing new experiences until it is my time to leave the physical world. I have to remain calm and grounded while learning in each new situation that I am faced with.

In a social setting, a man in his fifties came up to me and asked if I was a medium.

I proudly said, "Yes, I am."

He asked if I could talk to him. As he began to tell me his story, I could feel his sense of sadness—and that he wanted people to believe him. After his story, I was in awe. His life paralleled mine. He is gifted and has a connection to spirit, but no one ever believed him. He felt trapped and alone. The teasing had not stopped since he was a boy. I felt the burden lift as he explained his life to me. A six-foot-four-inch man with tears flowing down his cheeks revealed his life to me.

I told him that I was writing a book about my life, and it could help him with his. He did not feel alone after our talk. By the end of the evening, I realized that I was guided to that social event to help someone in need of spiritual help. I felt comfort in knowing that I could help and support someone, especially when no one else could.

It feels like that part has been a long learning curve for me. I am human, and I realize that I need to be able to do fun, human things in my life, but it does not always work that way. If a message is meant to come through, it comes through.

Before a reading, my family witnesses how I act. I am not myself at all. I feel spirits trying to connect. I have major anxiety. I may feel like I have spleen cancer, a heart attack, a gunshot to the back of my head, or a crushed chest from a car accident. It feels so good to sit down with the client and start the reading. I feel free and in my element. The pains begin to go away.

When I travel to other cities to do readings, I need a driver. My mind is not there to focus on the drive. My family has learned to understand me, and they grow with me through this spiritual process. They are very supportive and assist me in any ways they can. Knowing I have their support helps keep me focused on the work I need to do in the physical world. Most of my family is on the other side. My husband, daughter, and son are very special, and they mean the most to me here in the physical world.

CHAPTER 9

And My Mom Comes in to Raise Me from the Other Side

Once I accepted my gift as a medium, and especially when I started working as a medium, I had to begin a journey of self-healing. I have to be at my best—not packing burdens or carrying unresolved anger to be the best I can be. I have to be clear and completely full of love to share with the world. All my thoughts need to be positive without negativity creeping in. I have to be grounded and focused in the two worlds in which I live and love. I love to help people. I enjoy giving healing messages and watching a stranger's entire life transform in front of me.

The first step I had to take was looking at the relationship between my mother and me. It was not an easy task for me. I was very angry in the beginning. She passed away three years before I decided to focus on healing that relationship. Her last few years on this earth plane were not easy for her. I could hardly bear to watch her going through so much hardship. I had to peel away the layers and start from the beginning. I went back to when I was born and how our relationship began as mother and daughter.

I began by remembering how loved I was. It is something I knew my whole life—even in the troubled times. I knew the love that my mom had for me was real and from the heart. Sometimes she didn't know how to show it, but she always tried in the ways she knew. I have come to appreciate that aspect of her.

My mom and dad tried to become pregnant for thirteen years. When I arrived, our little town was so excited for my parents. It had been such a long wait. My life as a little girl in the physical sense was perfect. What more could I ask for than a loving family? Even if they didn't understand me sometimes, I always knew they were there for me through thick and thin. The perfect life turned to tragedy the day my father passed away. My mom was left all alone at the age of forty-six. She had to raise me by herself.

My father had been the sole provider; in those days, moms stayed home with the children. With the death of my father, she was forced to go to college, and she began working a job. She knew how important figure skating was to me. She made sure I was still able to do what I loved most. As time went on, she made many sacrifices for me. She was trying to play the role of mom and dad. As the stress became a larger burden, she turned to alcohol to numb the pain. She missed my father so much. When he passed, I felt like a part of her soul went with him. She was here physically on earth, but she was in a shell of her own body. She felt numb and lost. She had lost her best friend and soul mate, and on top of that, she had a ten-year-old to think about.

As time went on, it all became too much. The addiction to alcohol took over her life. My dad stepped in at that time to raise me from the other side. He and I both knew my mom could not be there for me. I had to rely on my dad to raise me. The addictive behavior started to take a toll on me. I begged her to stop. I began to blame myself, and I asked the what-ifs. If only I could be a better child, would she stop drinking? Maybe my craziness was wearing on her.

I started to replay different scenarios in my head. Is this something I caused? I needed to find answers. I found help in counseling and support groups. I understood the addicted person in my life, and I learned how to deal with the addiction instead of blaming myself.

When my daughter was born in 1995, my mom decided to seek the help she always needed. She chose to be a grandma—a clean and sober grandma. I was so proud of her. It is a big step to admit that you are an alcoholic and to ask for help. From that year on, she declared herself a recovering alcoholic, and she stayed sober until the day she passed away.

Through the tears, laughter, and anger, I was able to put myself on the healing journey. My mom began to come through in mediumship readings with healing messages. I received some personally and others from mediums I work with at workshops I host. My mom came through with apologies, jokes, and validation that she takes responsibility for her actions while she was in the physical world. She validated so many situations to prove she is with me at all times. Our love bond remains strong. She is in energy form, and I am energy in a physical body. Nothing can break our bond of love. She leaves me many signs through feathers and songs. Some days, I hear the song on the radio wherever I go. I even wake up with the song stuck in my head and can't shake it all day. I find feathers when I am not thinking about them, but that's when I need them the most. I smell her cigarette smoke from time to time in my house, and it is a nonsmoking house. She is making it very clear that she is parenting me from the other side along with my dad. She has joined the spiritual parenting team. I know that she is the mom from the other side that she could not be while she was here in the physical world. She had some tough lessons to endure while she was here in school.

We are all here on earth to learn lessons. Our souls are learning lessons. It is planned before we enter the schoolroom. The hardest times we go through here can be our greatest teachers. Our souls learn and grow the most in tough times—if we take responsibility and acknowledge our actions and what changes can be made to improve our lives so that we don't repeat the lessons. It's about learning to find the positive even when it doesn't seem like there is a light at the end of the tunnel.

We always face challenges—no matter who we are. How do we deal with them? Doors start to open for us when we are on the right path. Only you have the power to make this happen. What are you going to choose to advance in your life lesson? Once we cross over to the other side, we have a life review. We pull out a blueprint and see how did we do on earth. Did you fulfill your soul's journey that you set out to do in the beginning when you came down to school?

Apologies can happen in readings. Healing messages can come from the other side. Loved ones may feel like they owe an apology to those left in the physical world. Souls take responsibility for the mistakes they made while they were here and complete the journey. Perhaps more schooling on the other side is needed to complete the journey if it was not completed on earth. That is the opportunity that my mom took to apologize to me. Allowing it and accepting it into my life helped me in my healing journey. I began to heal, and I could see the positive in my relationship with my mom while she was here.

Challenges can make it hard to see the positives when everything looks like a gray, foggy mist. Our heads are not clear enough to make sense of our current situations. We allow the negatives to stick in our minds. It is not good for us since we have to continue the journey in the physical world. It is important to deal with the burdens we carry. It makes the journey so much lighter. You feel a sense of freedom, and you attract the positive people and things in your life that you need to help you along your path of life.

My mom and I have never had as good a relationship as we do now. I can even laugh and joke with her. When she wants her presence known, she makes sure it gets through. I love my mom, and I am so blessed to have been on this journey with her. I am so happy that she is raising me from the other side—along with my father! The best news is that I have two parents who love me and are always with me, guiding and directing me in the choices I need to make on my journey. It feels good to have two parents involved in my life; I only had that opportunity in the physical world until I was ten years old.

I miss their physical presence dearly. I miss being able to hug them—even a simple hug. At least I can be thankful that they are still around in spirit, seeing and supporting me as I continue my journey in the physical world.

C H A P T E R   1 0

The New Experience: Family Death as a Working Medium

I am living my so-called normal life as a human and a medium. I grow and advance in my spirituality on a consistent basis. As I learn and grow, so do new experiences. Just when I think I have it all figured out, something new happens. As a working medium, the deaths in my family have become new experiences. I am used of being called into action where I am physically in touch with a family member who is about to pass. As time has gone on, all of that has changed. I cannot explain the reason. I just go with the flow and follow how I am guided; sometimes I ask my guides questions when I don't understand why.

I was notified that an aunt on my dad's side and an aunt on my mom's side were both in the hospital. They lived miles apart from each other, and I didn't know which way to go. *Who do I assist?* As usual, I put all my daily things on hold to assist others. It is a part of my life that I have grown to adjust to. People always say, "Jody, you are too nice." I cannot be any other way—or I would not be me.

Jody Lutzke

As I carried on with my day, my cousin called. Her mom was not doing well. They were not sure where things were going. I dropped everything and made the hour-long drive to the hospital. When I arrived, family had gathered around my aunt's hospital bed. As I stood beside her bed, I let her know, through thought, what I was thinking. I told her I loved her and that she would be okay. I thanked her for all the fun times I had with her and my cousins growing up. I was recalling specific events that would make us all chuckle.

After a while, we were guided to a little sitting area in the hospital room. I sat with my back toward the wall and faced my aunt. I was having a conversation with other family members about life and catching up on the past few weeks. I was being an active listener, and I happened to glance over at my aunt. What I immediately witnessed was beyond what I had ever experienced before. I saw my aunt's soul leaving her physical body. Although she remained very close to her bedside, I saw her dancing with my uncle who had passed years before. I blinked and blinked again. *Am I seeing this right? I cannot believe it, and I have seen some crazy things.* My eyes were focused on what I was witnessing. Everything went quiet. I could not hear anything. It was like time stood still. I felt like I watched it going on forever, but in reality, it was probably a minute. It was so peaceful to watch. As I started coming back into my human mind, I realized that her soul was ready to go home. She was waiting for her physical body to die.

I felt my cousin staring at me. I looked at her and smiled. I did not know what to say or how to respond because I had completely missed what she was saying. It was an awkward moment to say the least. We started another conversation.

A little time passed, and I knew it was okay to leave. On the drive home, I kept replaying what I saw in my mind. I could hardly believe it. I arrived home late, went to bed, and woke up to a phone call from my cousin. My aunt had passed in the night. My heart sunk at first, but then I realized she was continuing the dance with her husband. How special was that? I witnessed their first dance in the spirit world.

I told my cousin that I was willing to do anything to help.

She stopped me and said, "I need to ask you something."

I knew what question was coming.

She said, "At the hospital yesterday, you seemed to be staring at something. I knew you were connecting, but I didn't want to ask at the time. I am curious now. What did you see?"

It was my moment of truth. I told her exactly what I saw and how precious it was to witness.

She said, "Jody, my parents loved to dance!"

I did not know that. I had never witnessed them dancing in the physical world. It immediately calmed my cousin to know that her parents were together on the other side.

It took me a few days to process the situation. I had so many questions for my care team in spirit, as I call them. *Why did I see that? Why did she not pass while I was there? Why was this passing so different?* The answers came to me over time. I am persistent and not very patient when it comes to getting the answers I want or need. I soon learned that I did not need to be present during her passing. As a transitioner, I was able to support her on her way to the other side. It was still a hard death to deal with.

As a medium, I know the other side is our home, and it is beautiful. It is a place where we reunite with our loved ones who we lost in the physical world. The earth is our school, and we come so our souls can learn and grow through life lessons. I know our souls are at peace on the other side when we return home. I struggle with the fact that I am also human living in a physical world. I live with my feet in two worlds. I am sad in the physical world when I miss the physical presence of a passed loved one. At the same time, I know they are okay on the other side. The struggle goes back and forth for me. I need to grieve like others, but how? I know they are okay, and they are back home. The struggle can be exhausting. I have to sit down and sort out the pieces. I dissect the situation and make some sort of sense of it all in both worlds.

Unfortunately, my story does not end there. On a September

evening, I received a call from a cousin. An aunt on my mom's side was not doing well. I had never dreamed about what I was about to experience. It was ten o'clock, and the hospital was almost four hours away. I have set boundaries so that I am not informed about when people are going to pass. I received confusing and scary messages as a child, and I asked that I not be informed beforehand.

I knew it was too late to leave. I decided to go in the morning. At that moment, I heard a voice saying, "Two hours." I knew I would not make it in time if she had two hours left before leaving the physical world. How could I relay that message to my cousin? I couldn't. I said, "It is too dark. There could be animals on the road. I will try to make it in the morning." I was so torn. I was again confronted with two worlds. *In what way should I go? What can I do?*

I began helping over the phone. I told the family to talk to her. I said, "Even if she is not physically responding, talk to her anyway. She hears you. Make sure you talk to her. Tell her what you want to say and what you feel the need to say."

I was texting messages to the family, and I did not realize the time. I had been on the phone for an hour and fifty-five minutes. It was getting late, and I got ready for bed. I proceeded with my nightly routine. As I turned on the tap in the bathroom, I stopped, paused, and looked in the mirror. I felt a soul trying to come into my space. At that moment, I felt my aunt. I stopped the running water. I closed my eyes and said, "Auntie, I am sorry that I cannot be physically there for you, but you know I love you. Why do I feel your soul leaving your physical body?"

The bathroom lights flickered, and I was startled. I picked up my phone to tell my daughter about what had happened and felt her soul coming into my space, giving me a hug and a kiss me on the cheek, and saying, "I've got to go."

I looked up and saw her soul disappearing into a tunnel of white light. I cried and yelled, "She just passed."

At that moment, I received a text message that my aunt had passed. As a human, I started to cry very hard. In the next breath, I thought, *What a beautiful experience.* As a medium, it was a beautiful experience. My aunt knew I wanted to be there so badly but couldn't make it on time. It was meant to be that way. I was not supposed to be physically there when she passed. She came to me instead. I felt honored, but at the same time, I was sad. I had lost a special aunt from the physical world. I was frozen in my bathroom for quite a while. It was like time stood still.

I have grown so much spiritually since I began working as a medium. I don't have to hide anymore. I choose who I want to explain my experiences to. Most times, I explain them to anyone who will listen. It is amazing and healing at the same time. I help heal family members by being honest with what I experience. They knew she was at peace and that her passing was calm and flawless.

For several weeks, I kept remembering the amazing experience my aunt allowed me to have with her. It is another chapter in my life. I am grateful for the experience. I hear her voice and see her smile. I miss her physical presence, but I know she is okay on the other side. If I allowed myself to pack a burden from this experience I could.

For several months, I had tried to visit my aunt. My obligations to another sick member of my family kept me in my own town. My aunt put others before her. When I called to see how she was doing, she replied, "Don't worry about me. The other family member you are caring for is worse off than me. You tend to her."

Those are the last words I heard from her. I have to remind myself that it all happened the way she wanted it to happen. That is the way the story was a supposed to go. When the universe lines itself up for the way things are meant to be, there is no changing that. We are not powerful enough to change things when they are supposed to go a certain way.

All I can do is smile and honor her, the experience, and the lesson I learned from that situation. As for now, I will attend to my sick mother-in-law.

C H A P T E R　1 1

How to Help Yourself with Your Spiritual Gift

Acknowledging and admitting that I had a spiritual gift was the first step I needed to take on my journey in the physical world. Recognize that it is okay to be different—and admit it. I was willing to share it with anyone who needed my support and guidance in the physical world. I knew this was my path. Fear, as always, tried to come in. Fear comes from the ego. The ego tells us that we are not good enough and cannot handle the task at hand. The ego loves to bring fear into the equation. I had to be fully aware of that to keep it from blocking my way.

After coming out of the spiritual closet and starting my business, I knew I had to find new ways to cope with the energy flow. For me, it is about following my gut feelings. They guide me toward making the correct choices.

The first step in being open to receiving help, support, and guidance is to admit that you are gifted. It is time to acknowledge that you are different and that you have had spiritual experiences. It is about trusting yourself, believing in yourself, and owning your power. No one can ever take that power away from you—unless you allow them to. Believe in your power and strength, and the universe will guide you to where you need to go.

As a spiritual teacher, it is my job to teach, support, and help those who come to me for readings. Some of them learn they are gifted. The universe has given me and my spiritual team the job of teaching. People are guided to me by the universe, and they discover the potential they have. It gives them an opportunity to learn and grow with their gifts.

When a person begins to pursue a spiritual path and look at their gifts, fear can lurk around. A part of the human ego comes into play. It tells you that you can't or that you are not good enough. As you start to practice in spirituality, you will learn how to decipher whether it is the ego at play or if you are truly receiving messages.

Do you wake up full of energy, but by the end of the day, you have lost all of your energy, feel drained, and are left with many aches, pains, and symptoms you cannot explain?

When we are gifted, we have a beautiful bright white aura around our physical bodies. People with negative energy can physically drain our energy. That can leave you feeling exhausted. The negative energies are a lower energy, and they seek out white-light energy to keep themselves energized. Coming from a white-light source with a positive, loving energy, we need to protect ourselves. To protect yourself from being drained, you need to cover a few simple steps: grounding, shielding and protecting.

Grounding allows you to connect to Mother Earth and the cosmic energies above. It leaves you as the one—the vessel in the middle between the two. One is omnipresent energy. You are now the channel. You are rooted, and you can pull on Mother Earth's energies while connecting to cosmic energies.

When you wake up, put your feet on the ground. Think of growing roots, like tree roots out of the bottom of your feet, going deep into Mother Earth. Take a deep breath from Mother Earth and feel the clean, purified air coming all the way up through your physical body. Allow yourself to feel that pure, loving energy.

Loudly, release all the toxins from inside your body that no longer serve your purpose. Blow the air out of your mouth with a big gasp. You are now grounded!

Immediately ask for white-light protection. It is called shielding. Ask for white-light protection. Imagine a large white circle outlining your aura. Your aura is the energy field around your physical body. It looks like an oblong white circle around you. The white-light protection is full of love. It is creating and protecting a sacred space for you. In the physical world, you do not like people getting into your space, right? You can feel overwhelmed when people get in your face or your space. It works the same way with spirituality. You need to create a space where you feel protected and in control. You are owning your own power by doing so.

Protection is the next step. Ask to be protected in your sacred space. Setting boundaries is the key to protection. Be clear about what your intent to the universe, your guides, and the angels. Be specific: "This is my sacred space—and only mine—everyone, stay clear until I invite you in." You will feel your power. It is your space, and you will maintain your energy in there. By doing so, no one can siphon your energy and leave you feeling depleted. You will learn to maintain and keep your energy in your sacred space.

By following these steps, you will immediately feel a change in yourself. You will feel energized, refreshed, and in control! As you grow spiritually, your physical body will feel more refreshed and positive! You owe it to yourself to make your journey in the physical world a happy, positive, fun-filled adventure! Trust and believe in yourself—and never give up!

About the Author

Jody Lutzke is an established spiritual medium who began working professionally after starting her own practice in 2014. After a lifelong journey of hiding her spiritual gift, Jody embraced her identity and began delivering healing messages to those in the physical world and traveling wherever she is called to go. The small medium is full of spunk and charisma; her beauty resonates from the inside out as she shares her message with the world. Her focus is to bring peace and healing through her stories and experiences to assist others on their journeys.

Jody was raised in Fernie, British Columbia. By the age of two, she was connecting with spirits. Her family members recall her communicating with imaginary friends on a regular basis. Though she was often teased for it, she always believed in what she saw. At the age of ten, she had to deal with the death of her father. For years, death was a prominent part of her life. She lost many family members. When a close friend's nephew died in an accident, Jody revealed her lifelong secret. She was ready to step forward and share her amazing ability to connect with the other side.

Jody's goal is to bring an understanding and awareness to the friends and families that are left here to grieve the loss of loved ones. By delivering healing messages, Jody helps bring closure to those who are wounded or carrying burdens. Your loved ones are always with you. They know, see, guide, and protect you as you continue your journey in the physical world.

Jody has an associate's degree and worked in psychology and social work for many years before embracing her true self.

Printed in the United States
By Bookmasters